D1028794

Johann Sebastian Bach

TWO- AND THREE-PART INVENTIONS

Johann Sebastian Bach

TWO- AND THREE-PART INVENTIONS
FACSIMILE OF THE AUTOGRAPH MANUSCRIPT

With an Introduction by Eric Simon

Dover Publications, Inc., New York

Published in Canada by General Publishing Company, Ltd., 30 Lesmill Road, Don Mills, Toronto, Ontario.

This Dover edition, first published in 1968, contains a photographic reproduction, original size, of the facsimile of the autograph manuscript of J.S. Bach's *Two-and Three-Part Inventions* originally published by C. F. Peters, Leipzig (n.d.) and an Introduction to the present volume, written especially for Dover by Eric Simon. All translations in the Introduction are by Mr. Simon.

NOTE: The present printing (1978) omits the reprint of the *Inventions* from the Bach-Gesellschaft edition, and the General Editor's Preface, both of which appeared in the 1968 version.

International Standard Book Number: 0-486-21982-8
Library of Congress Catalog Card Number: 68-11918

Manufactured in the United States of America
Dover Publications, Inc.
180 Varick Street
New York, N.Y. 10014

INTRODUCTION TO THE DOVER EDITION

"Sincere instruction wherewith amateurs of the clavier, in particular the ones avid to study, are shown a distinct manner not only (1) to learn how to play cleanly with two voices, but also in the course of further progress (2) to deal correctly and nicely with three obbligato parts; at the same time, not only to get good *inventiones* of their own, but also to develop them well; mostly, however, to achieve a singing manner of playing, and along with it to receive a strong foretaste of composition. Made by Joh. Seb. Bach, Capellmeister of the Grand-Prince of Anhalt-Cöthen. A.D. 1723."

This is Bach's modest title for his *Fifteen Inventions and Fifteen Symphonies,* commonly called the *Two-* and *Three-Part Inventions,* respectively. These thirty little gems occupy a singular place in our keyboard literature. Although intended by the composer merely as exercise and training material, they have accompanied every pianist and harpsichordist, amateur and professional alike, from his early years through his whole life as a never-ending source of pleasure and object for study. They are played by the reluctant beginner as well as by the accomplished concert artist in his recitals. With Bach's *Well-Tempered Clavier* and Beethoven's thirty-two sonatas they constitute the pianist's Bible.

Unlike the *Well-Tempered,* the *Inventions* do not cover all the major and minor keys in chromatic order. Keys with a signature of more than four sharps and flats, two keys with four (A-flat major and C-sharp minor), and one key with three (F-sharp minor) are omitted, sparing the beginner undue hardships.

The *Inventions* were first written down in the *Little Clavier Book for Wilhelm Friedemann Bach,* an exercise book intended for the composer's son and marked, "Started at Cöthen, January 22, 1720." Here the *Inventions* can be found in their original form together with additional works of Bach and other composers, entered partly by Bach himself,

partly by some pupils. This manuscript is now owned by the Music Library of Yale University in New Haven. A second manuscript, not from J. S. Bach's hand, shows several changes and improvements, but also obvious errors. In 1723 the composer's continuous work on his *Inventions* had progressed so far that he was able to write a fair copy incorporating the teaching experience of several years and representing his final intentions. This last manuscript, as well as the second one, is in the possession of the Berlin State Library, and is reproduced in this publication.

Only few of Bach's works were printed during his lifetime, and in spite of their musical and educational importance the *Inventions* were first published by Hoffmeister & Co., Leipzig, in 1801, half a century after the composer's death.

Serious readers may want to compare the present facsimile with the printed version in the famous Bach-Gesellschaft edition, based on this very autograph. It was the intention of the Gesellschaft editor, Carl Ferdinand Becker, to convey a faithful copy of the manuscript by not adding dynamic and phrasing marks, a common but dubious usage of later editions, and by even refraining from adding slurs where, by analogy with corresponding passages, they were clearly intended. He brought the *Inventions* orthographically up to date; this included the following changes:

1. Whereas Bach used soprano, alto and bass clefs, but not the treble clef, Becker used only treble and bass clefs.

2. Becker indicated the sharps and flats of the key signature only once, whereas Bach wrote them in all places of the staff where they applied; thus, for example, in the manuscript the F-sharp in the left hand of the seventh two-part invention in E minor can be found under the staff and on the fourth line. Since Bach follows this procedure consistently in this

« *Explication* unterschiedlicher Zeichen, so gewisse *Manieren* artig zu spielen, andeuten. »

FIG. 1. Bach's explanation of ornaments. Above: Page 8 of the autograph manuscript of the *Clavier-Büchlein vor Wilhelm Friedemann Bach* (from the reproduction published by the Yale University Press, 1959). Below: The same explanation as printed on page xiv of Volume III of the Bach-Gesellschaft edition of Bach's works. (*Steigend* = ascending; *fallend* = descending.)

work, we should not be surprised to find in the manuscript a piece in E major with six sharps, a piece in E-flat major with four or five flats, depending on the clef, etc.

3. Whereas Bach writes a dotted note across a bar line, putting the note on the left of the bar line and the dot on the right (see the eighth and seventh bars from the end of the third two-part invention), Becker ties the main note (in this case an eighth) to the note of half its value (in this case a sixteenth) in the next measure.

4. Whereas Bach connects the ledger lines of adjacent notes (see the second line of the fifth two-part invention), Becker separates them.

Let us not be confused by notes showing through from the reverse side of a manuscript page, as, for example, in the first measure of the second page of the ninth two-part invention.

In the manuscript of the first two-part invention we find many groups of two sixteenth-note triplets, as exemplified in the first measure on the second quarter of the right hand and the fourth quarter of the left hand. The middle notes of these triplets were obviously added later, perhaps not by Bach himself, in order to produce a technically more challenging version. The published edition starts with the first invention in its simpler version, while the "triplet version" is added at the end.

According to Bach's son, Carl Philipp Emanuel, all grace notes were written in his father's time as eighths regardless of their actual value, and therefore have to be interpreted according to the prevailing tradition and musical exigencies, an often controversial matter not to be elaborated on at this point. However, we would like to reproduce the elder Bach's own "Explanation of divers symbols which indicate how to perform certain ornaments properly" from his *Little Clavier Book for Wilhelm Friedemann Bach* (Figure 1).

We consider it of great importance to say a few words about the phrasing of the *Inventions*. We find only two (two-part, Nos. 3 and 9) with numerous slurs, and only three (two-part, Nos. 2 and 15; three-part, No. 9) with a few solitary ones. Does that mean that most of the *Inventions* should be chopped away

in a non-legato kind of playing as you may often hear it done by pianists proud of playing the "Urtext"? Certainly not. We must never forget that these pieces, according to Bach's title, quoted at the beginning of this preface, were designed "mostly . . . to achieve a singing [*cantable*] manner of playing." Therefore it is obvious that Bach did not intend *only* the passages marked by slurs to be played legato; rather, the slurs exemplify where and how a legato should be executed. Even so, there are reasons to be careful and thoughtful. Let us have a look at the third two-part invention in D major, which Bach most lavishly endowed with slurs. The Gesellschaft editor, Becker, attempted to reproduce Bach's manuscript as faithfully as possible. But does Bach, in the first and second measure, really mean the phrase to start only on the second sixteenth? Or, as in all the following instances, would the little bow, whatever its exact length and position, not rather apply to the entire measure? More than that: we never see a slur extended beyond one measure. Could it be that Bach meant measures 5—9 to be played "under one bow"? Or look at the staccato dots in measures 5 and 33, faithfully reproduced by Becker. As no other staccato dot can be found elsewhere in the entire work, may they not be interpreted as an accident of the quill or of nature?

All these questions are well worth asking, and through the present edition we hope to make the discussion as wide and as fruitful as possible.

As an afterthought, we suggest that, as an exercise in clef and manuscript reading, a student should use the manuscript for playing, after having practiced any one of these *Inventions,* of which Albert Schweitzer says: "If the average musician of our days may have less knowledge of the theory of composition, but certainly a much greater understanding of the distinction between true and false art, we owe this primarily to these pieces of Bach. The child who has once practiced them, as mechanical as the procedure may have been, has acquired a perception of part-writing unable to be erased. Instinctively he will look in every composition for a similarly masterful weaving of the voices, and feel the poverty of the music where it is lacking."

ERIC SIMON

Johann Sebastian Bach

TWO- AND THREE-PART INVENTIONS

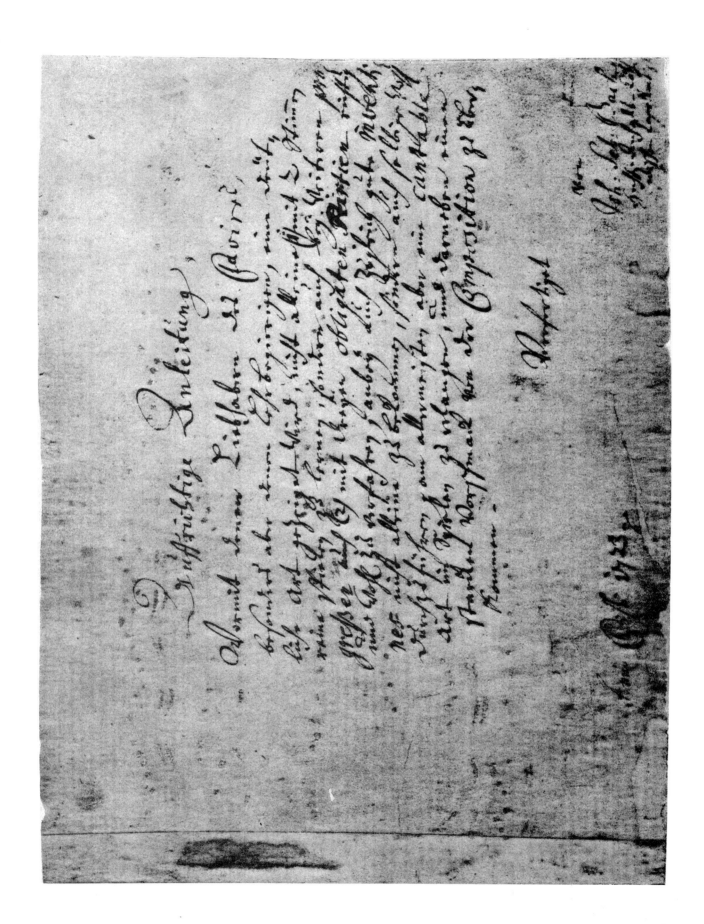

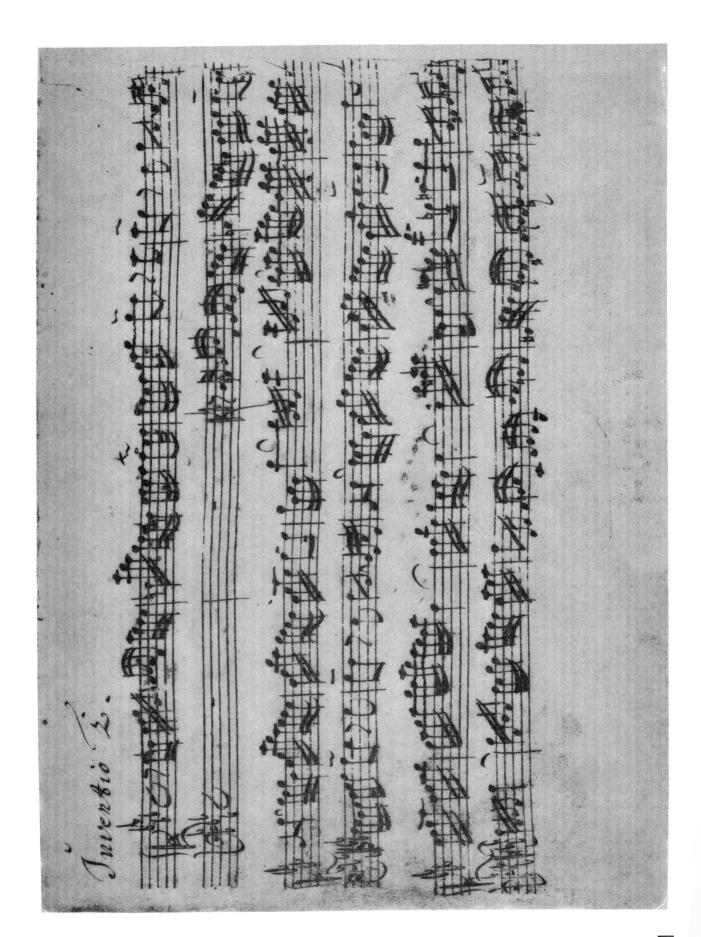

[4]

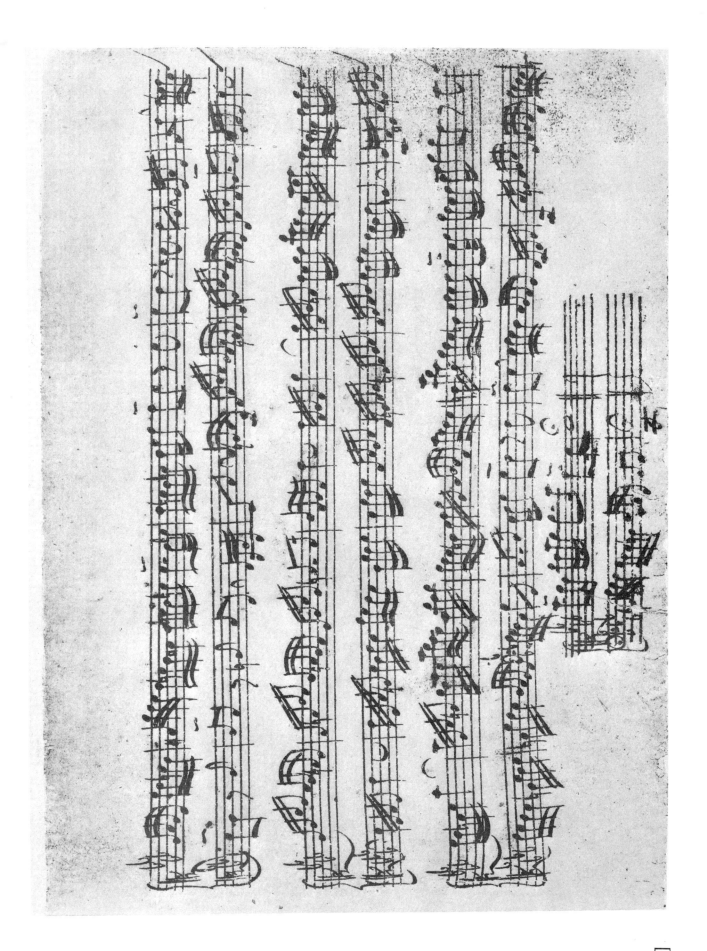

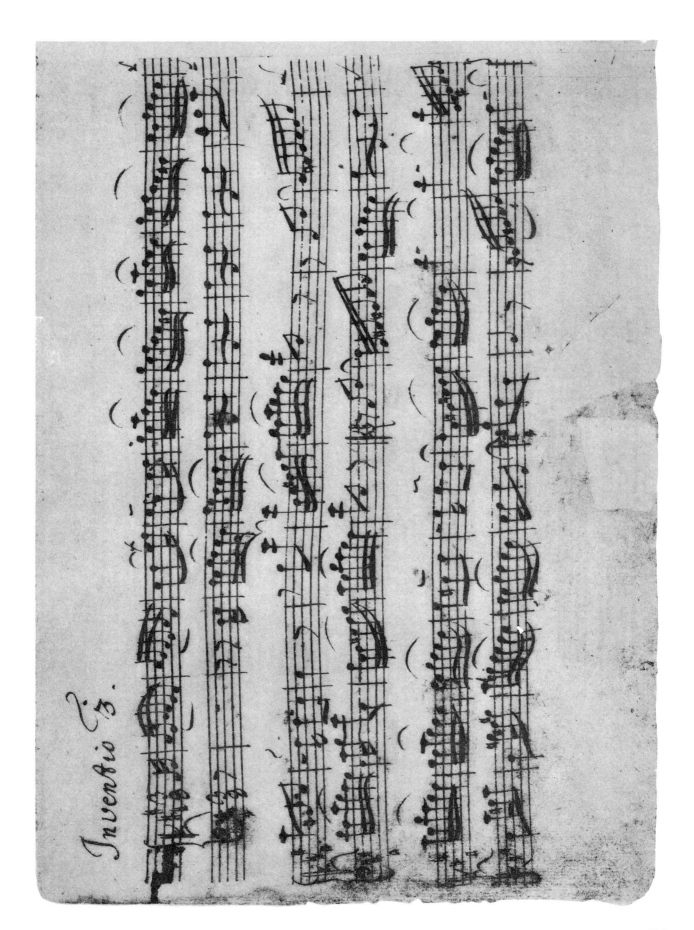

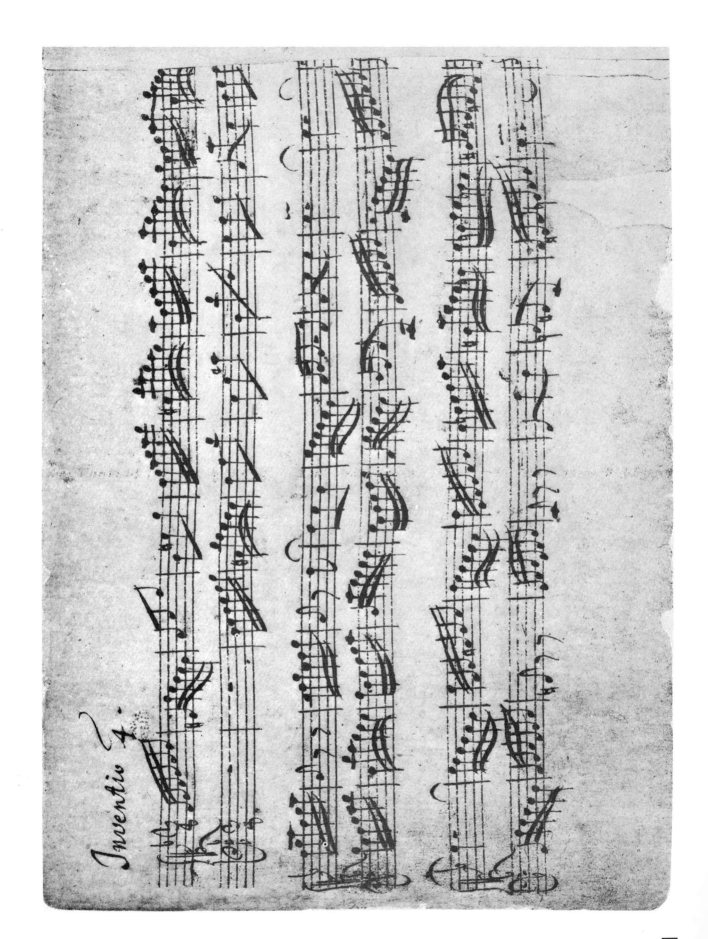

Inventio 7.

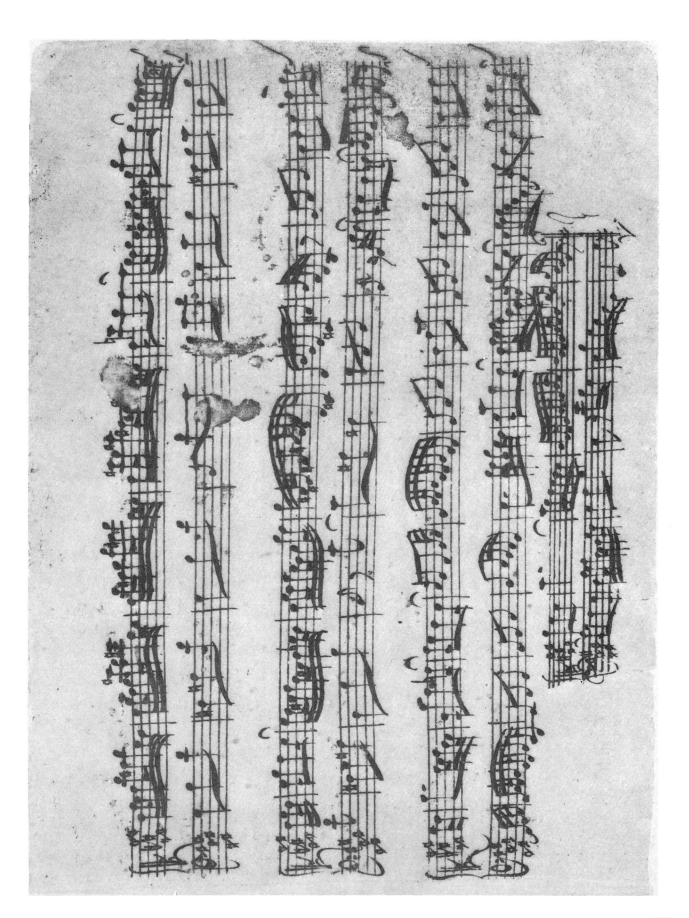

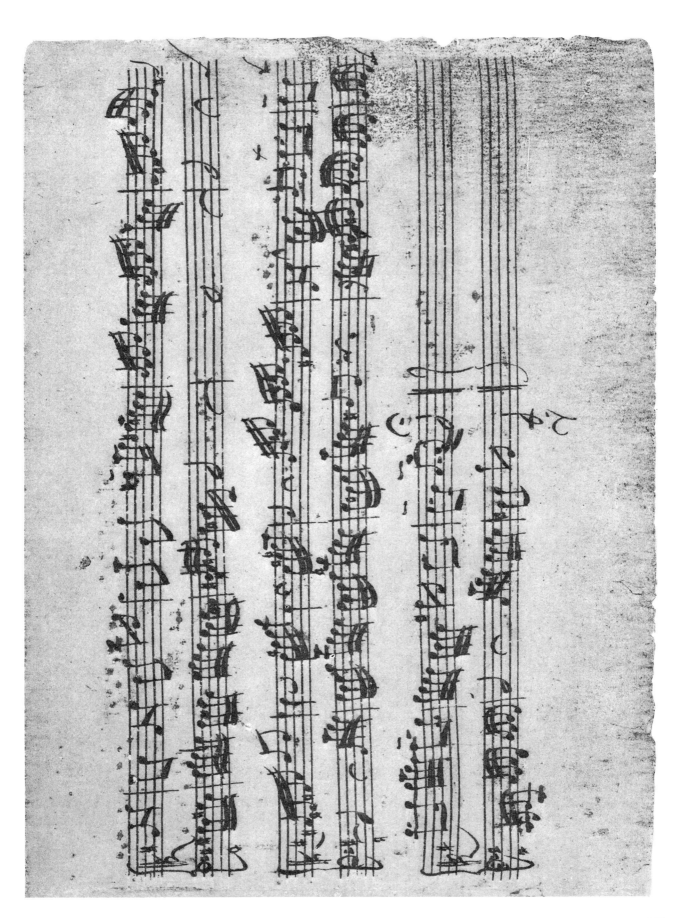

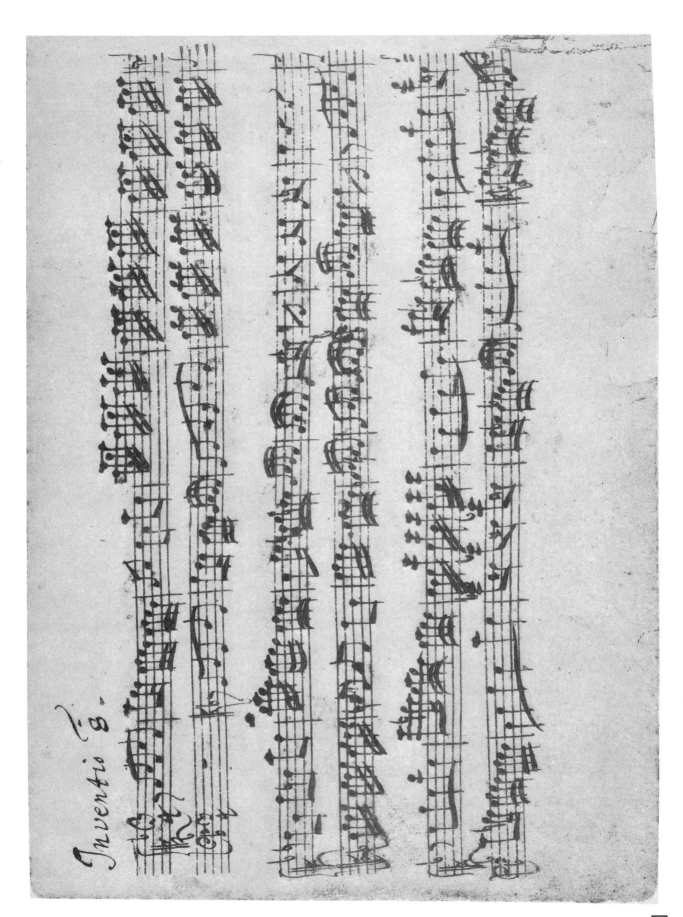

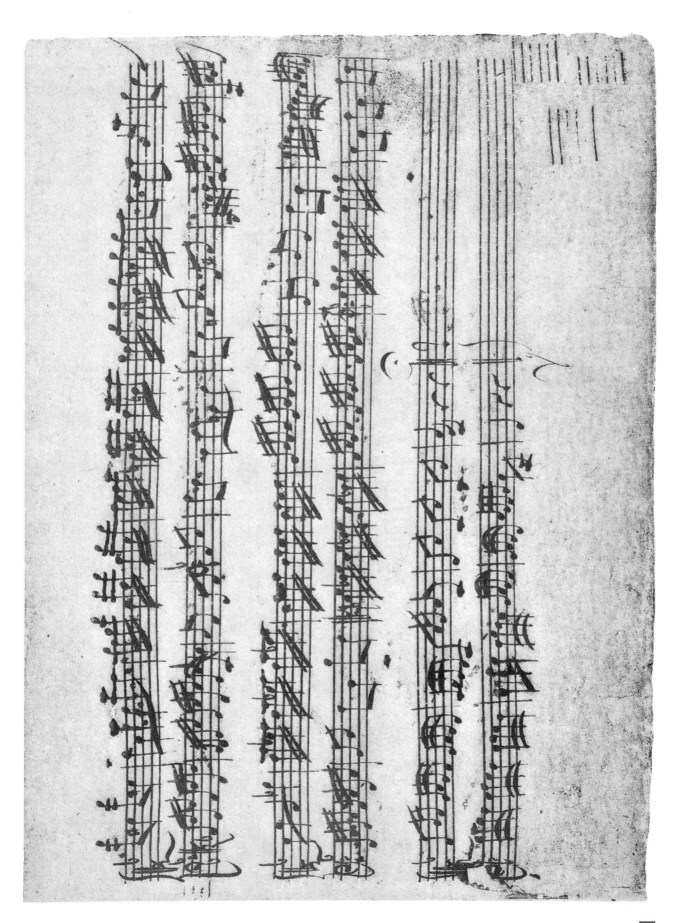

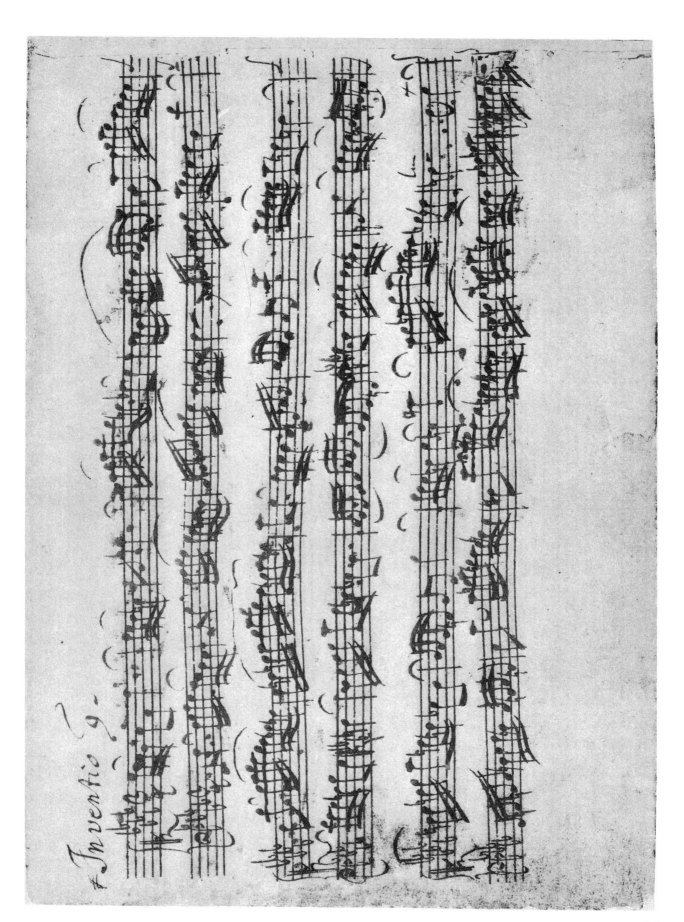

Inventio 9.

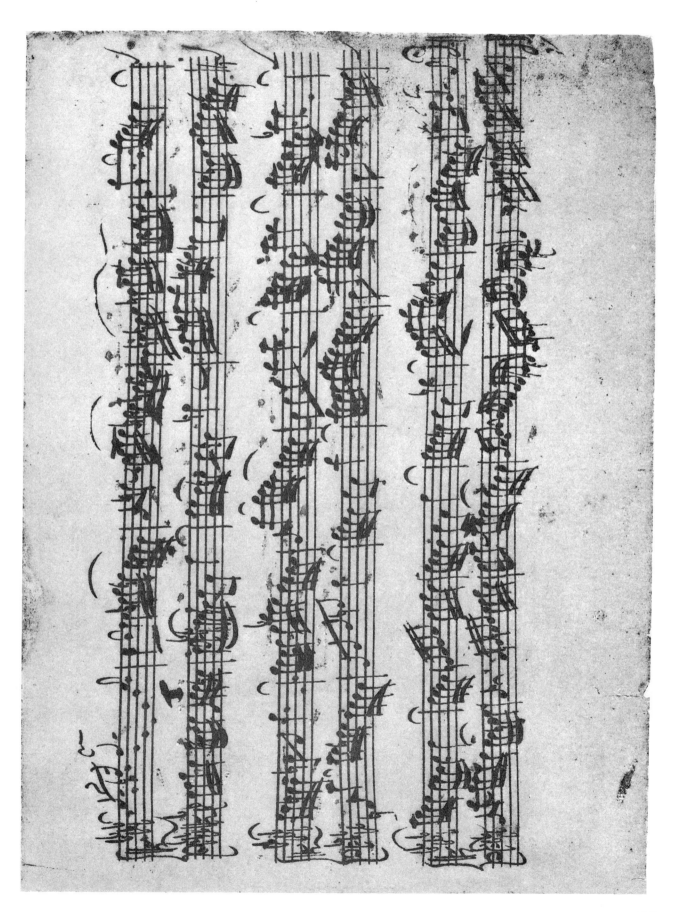

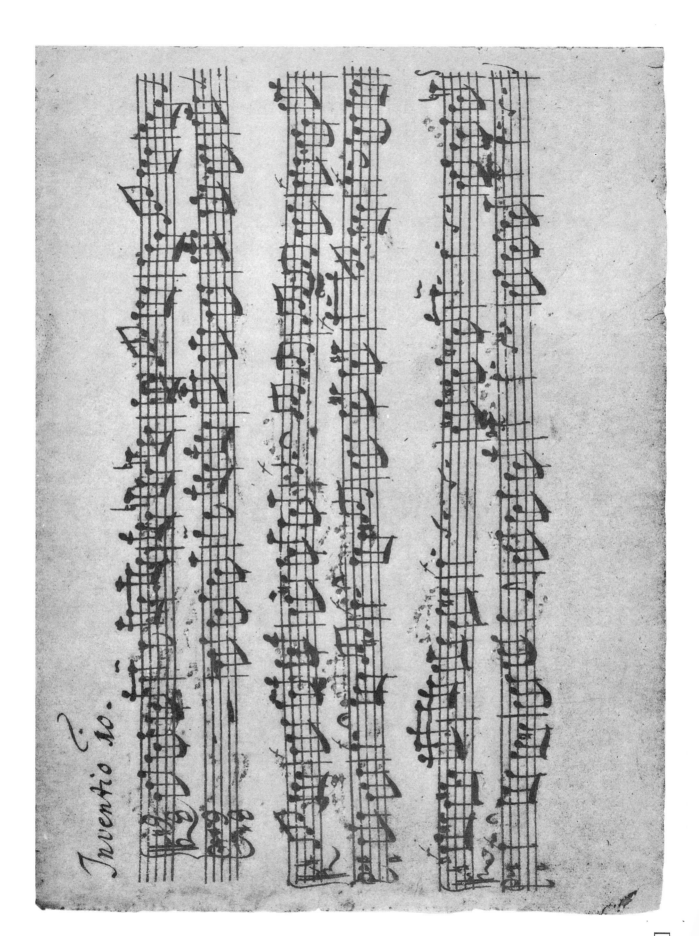

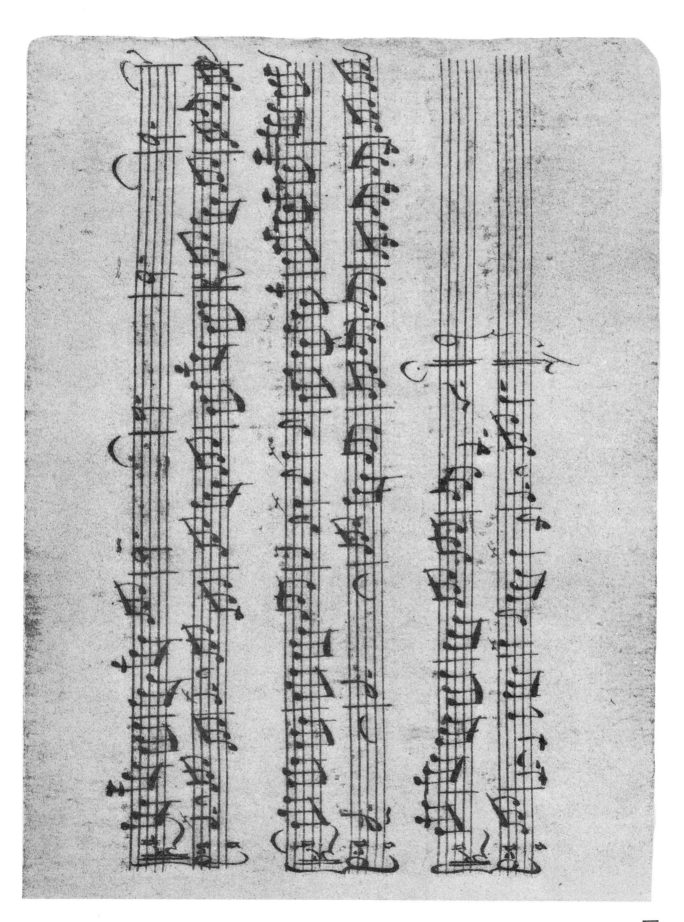

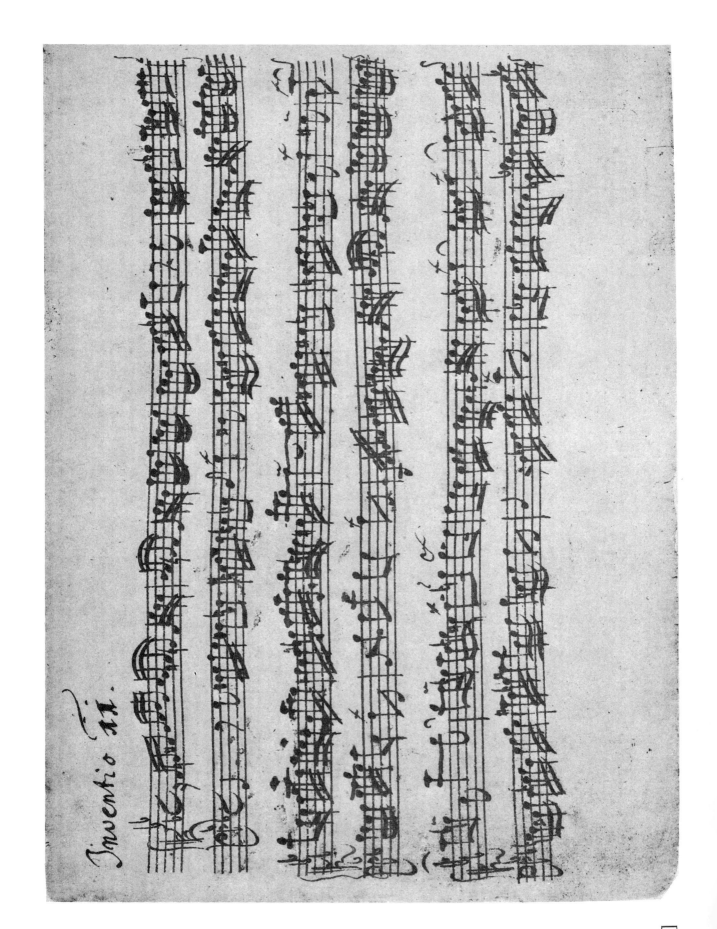

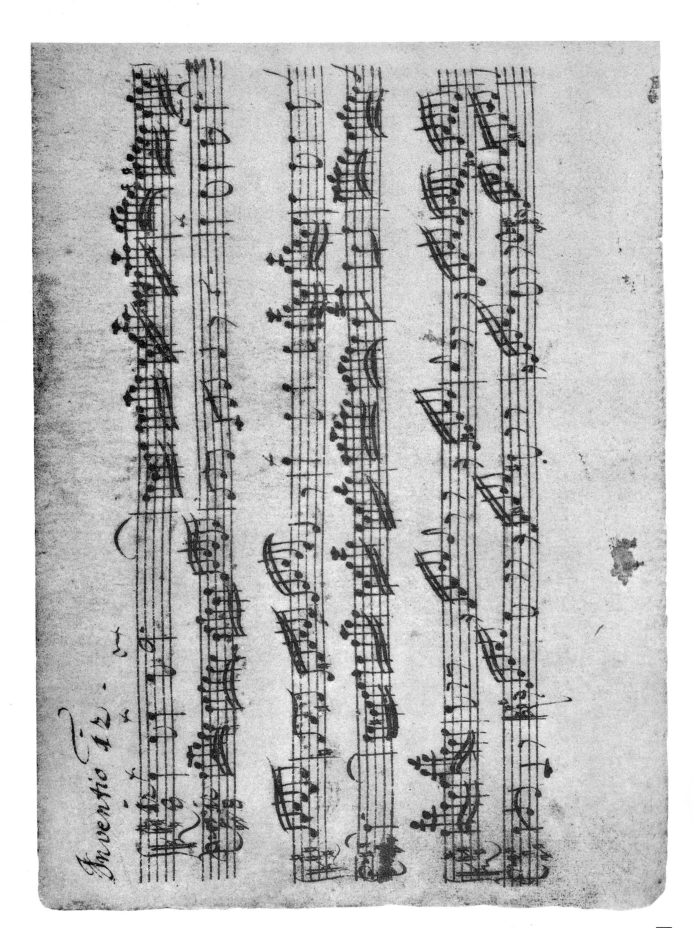

[24]

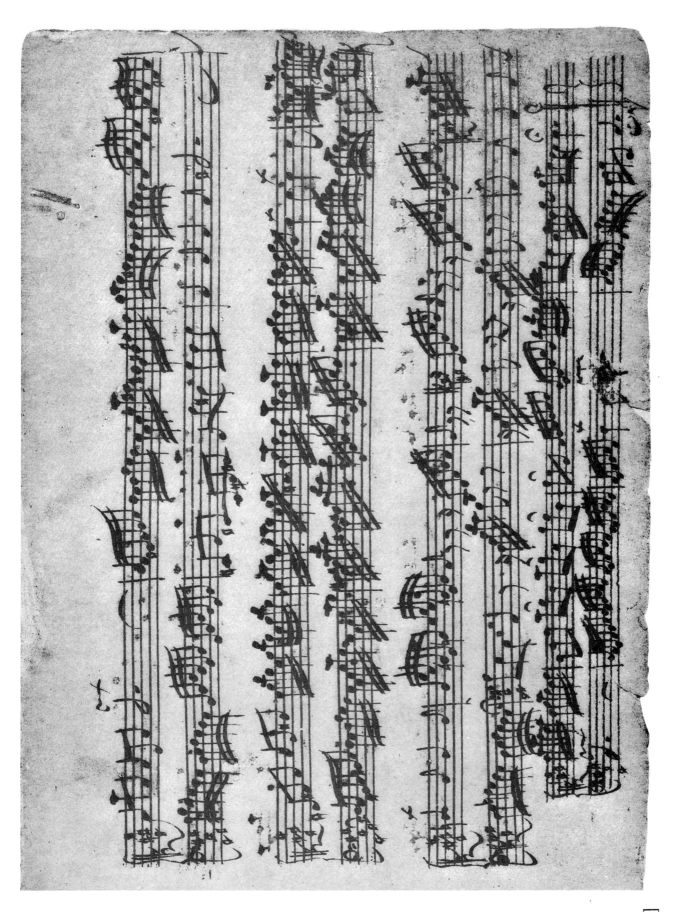

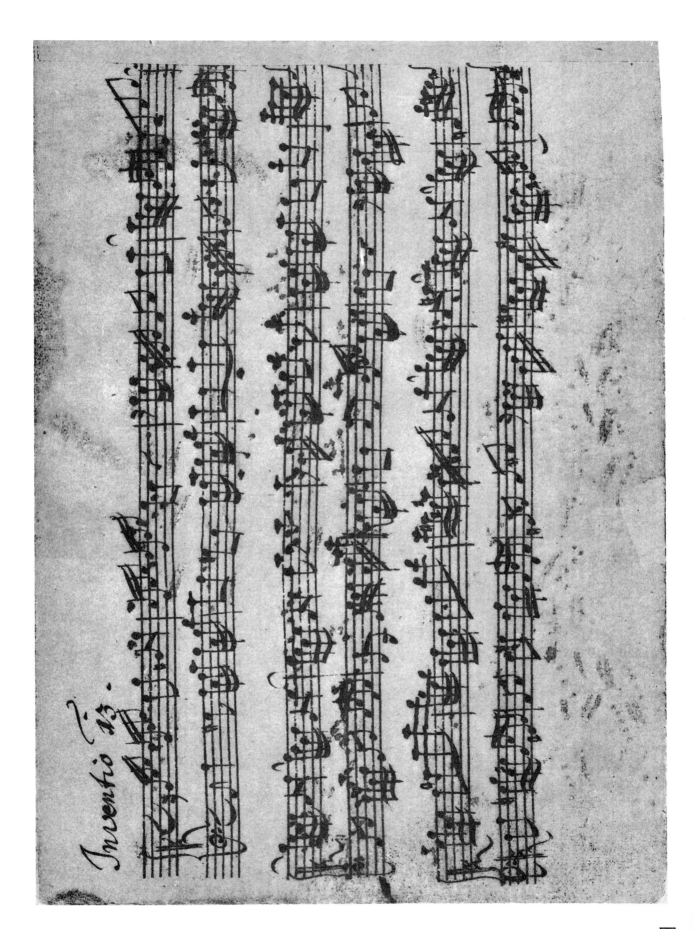

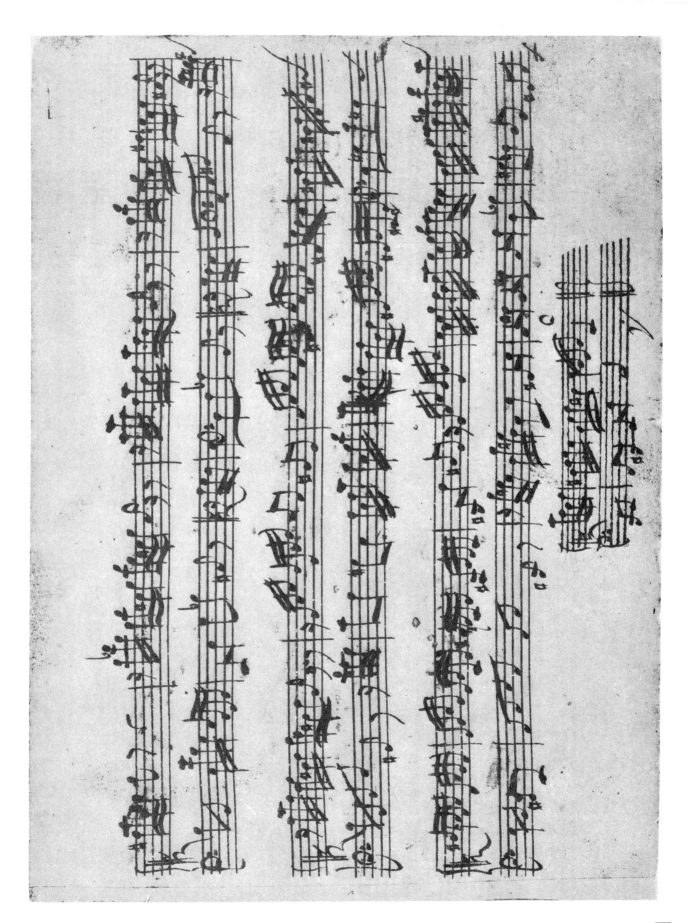

Inventio 14

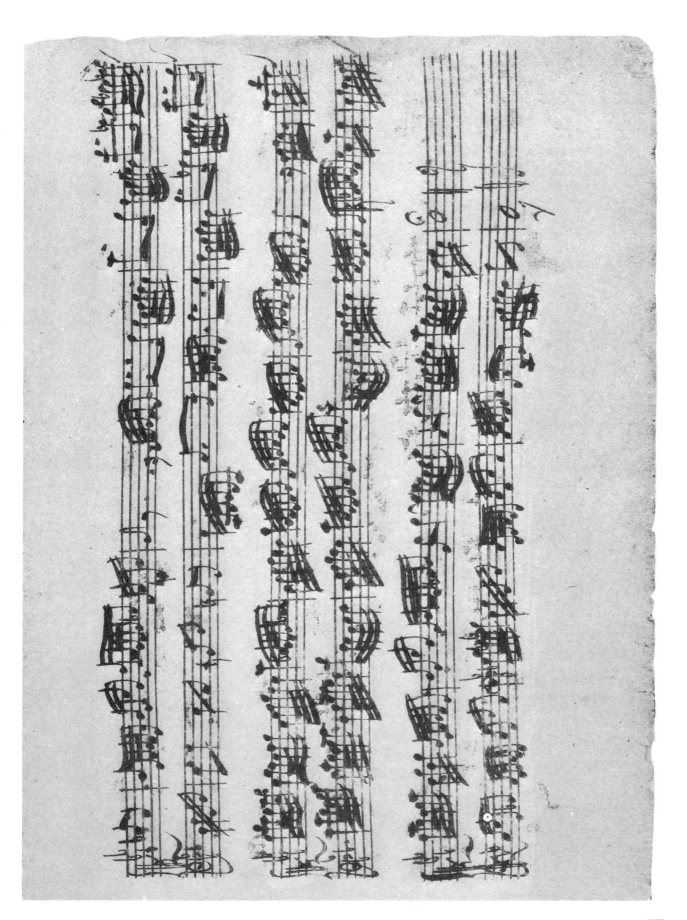

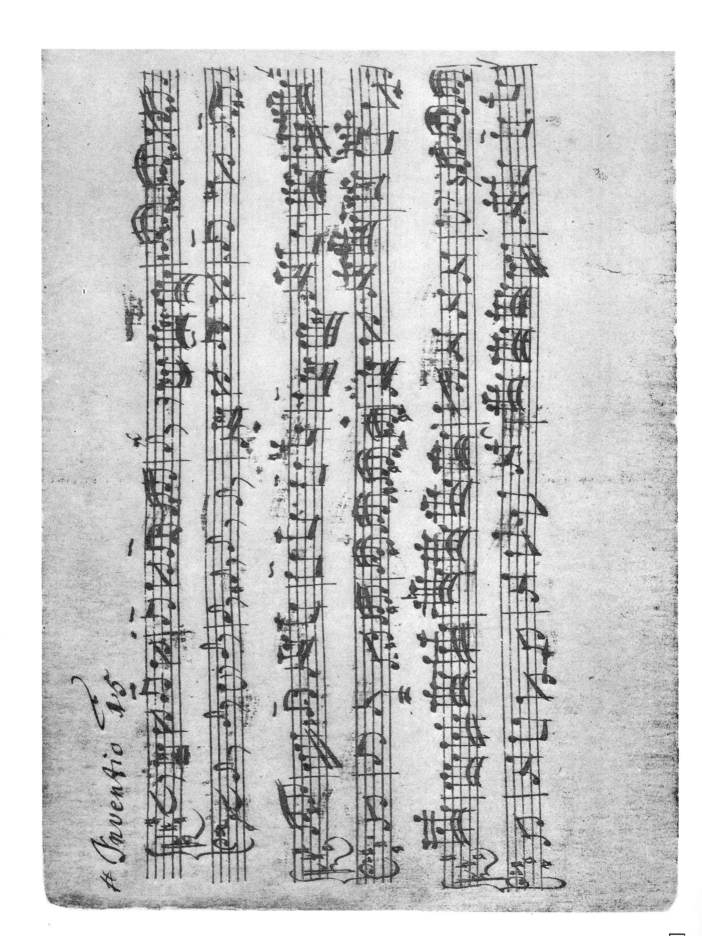

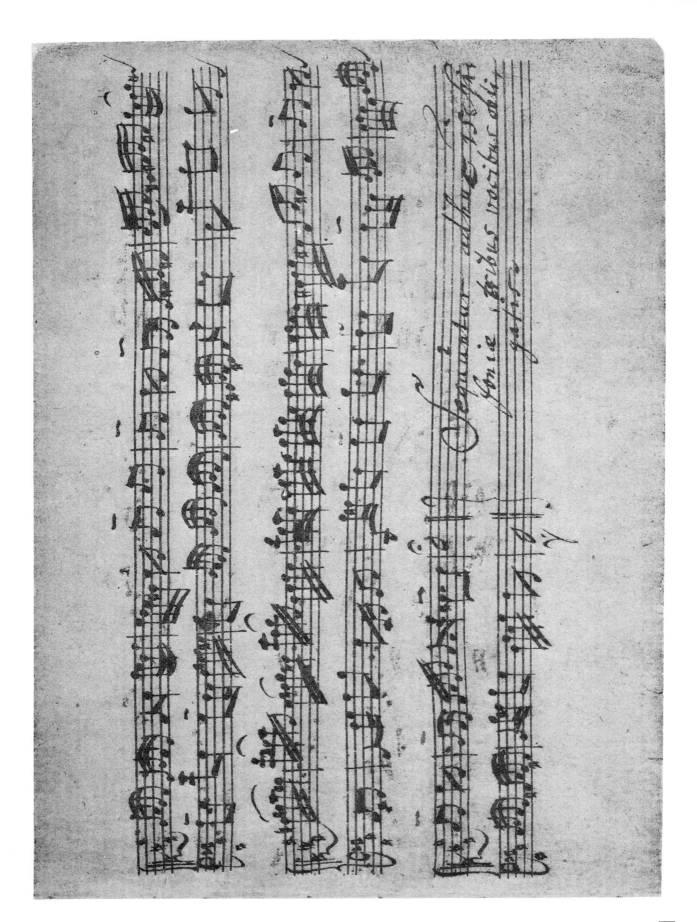

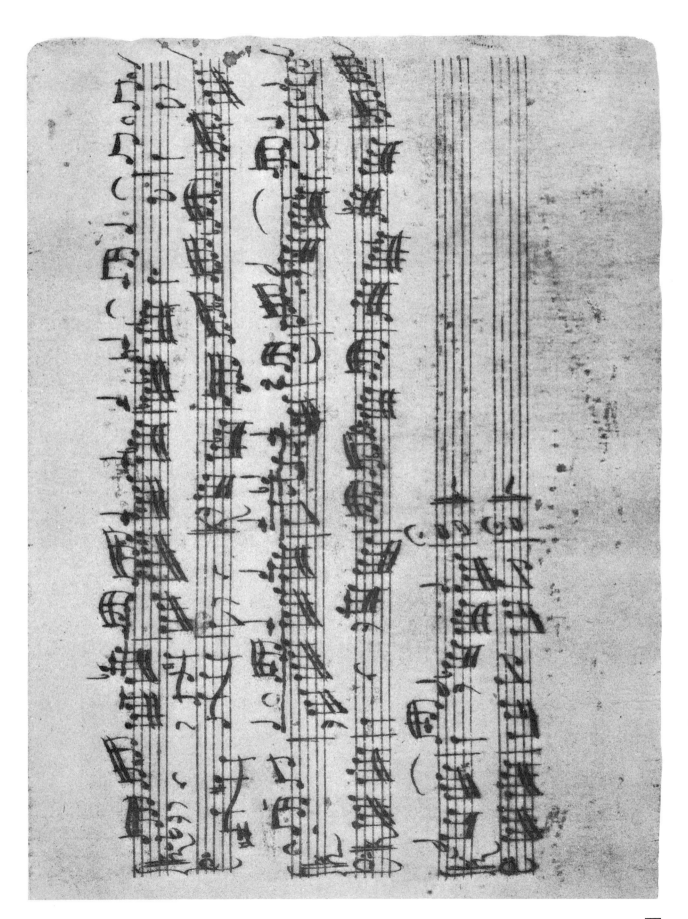

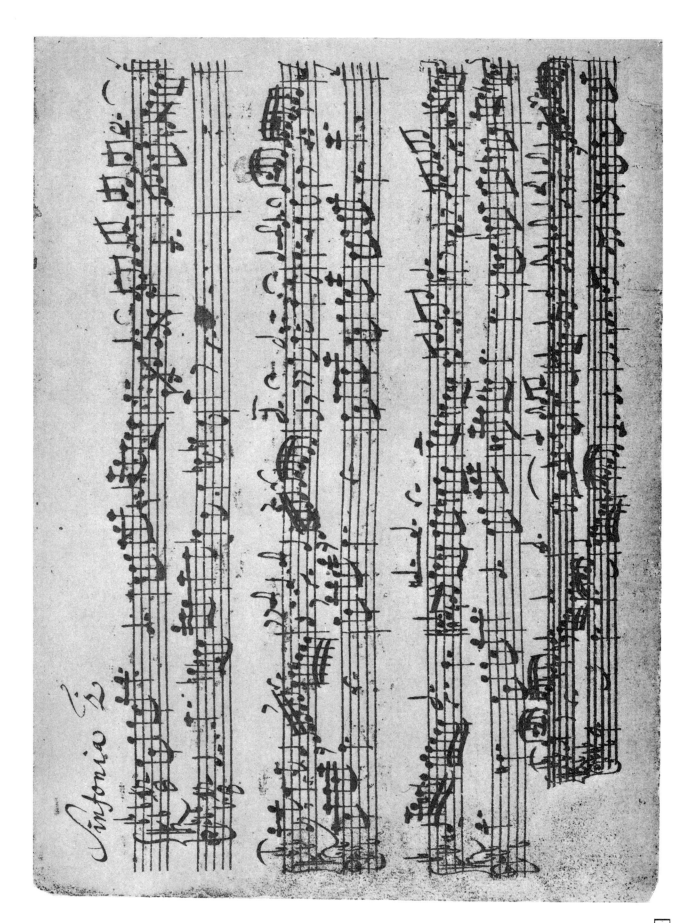

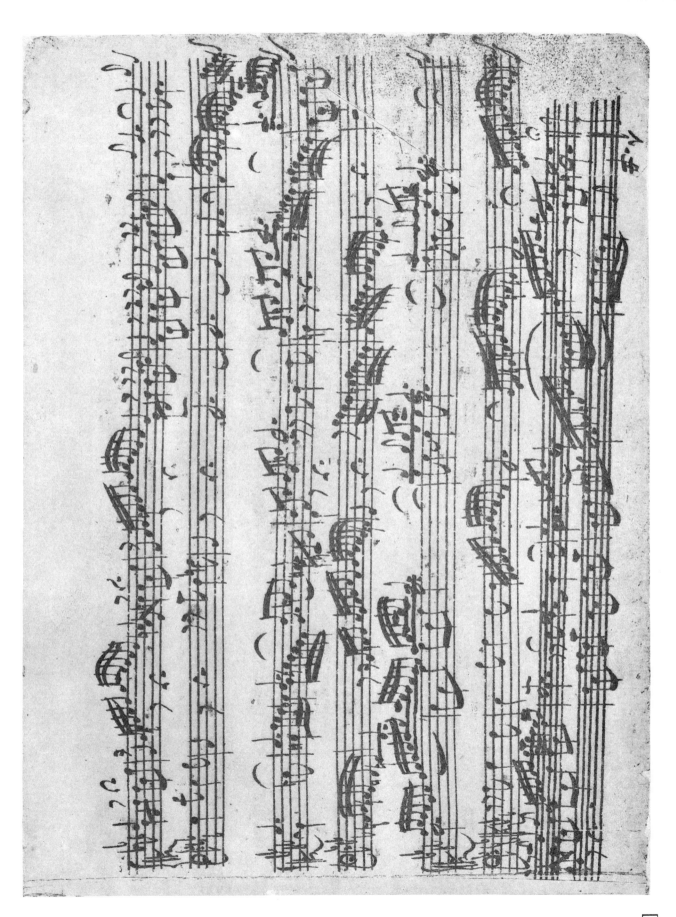

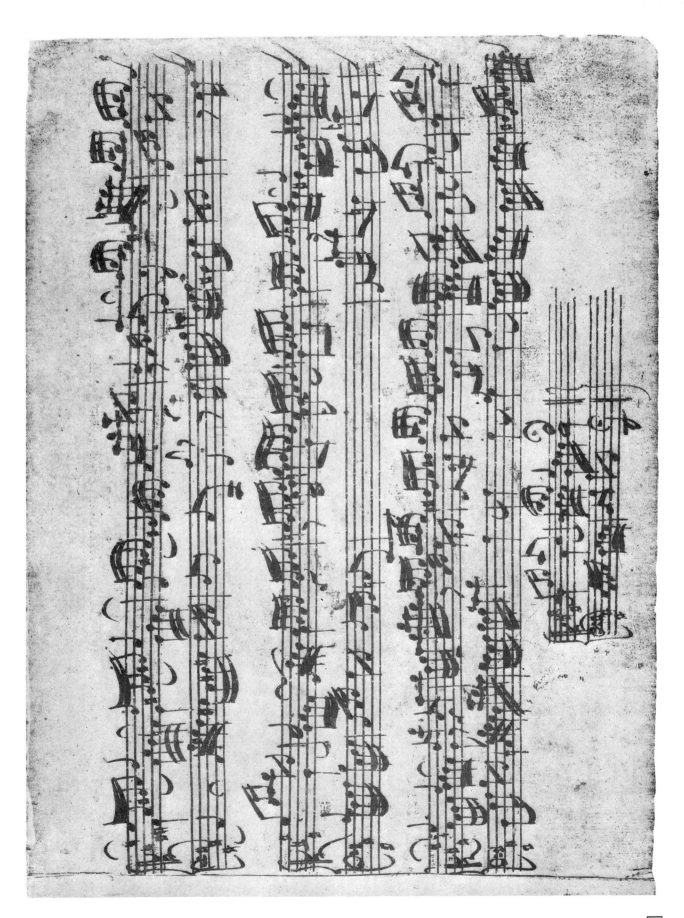

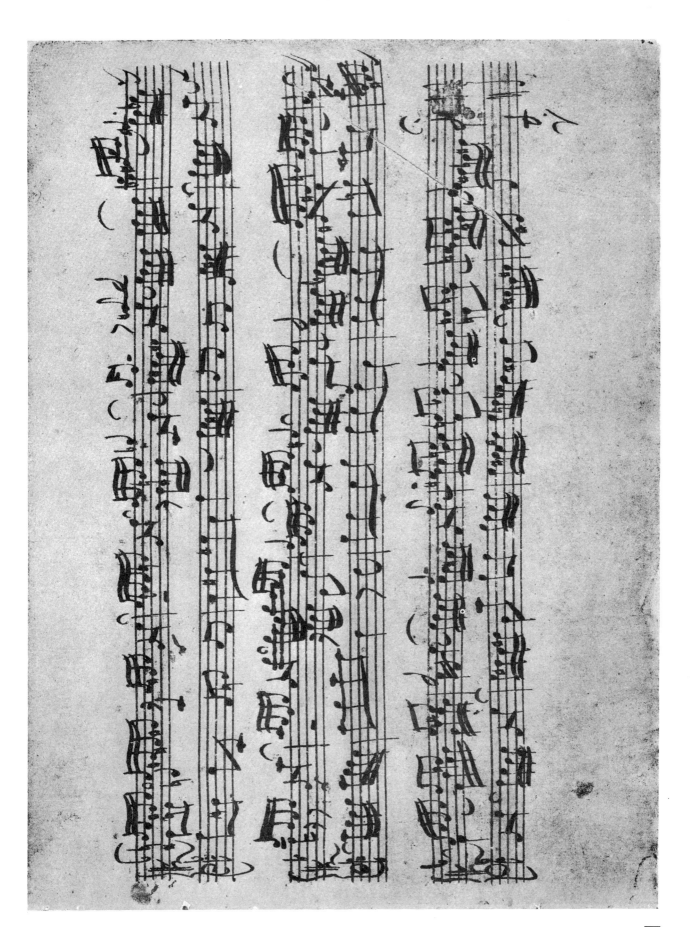

[39]

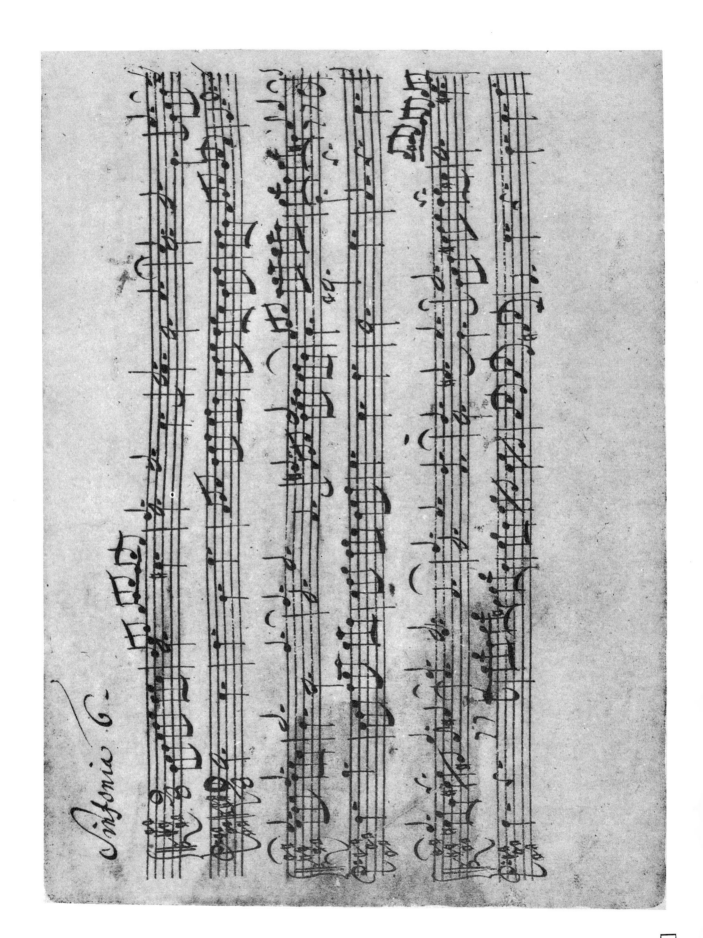

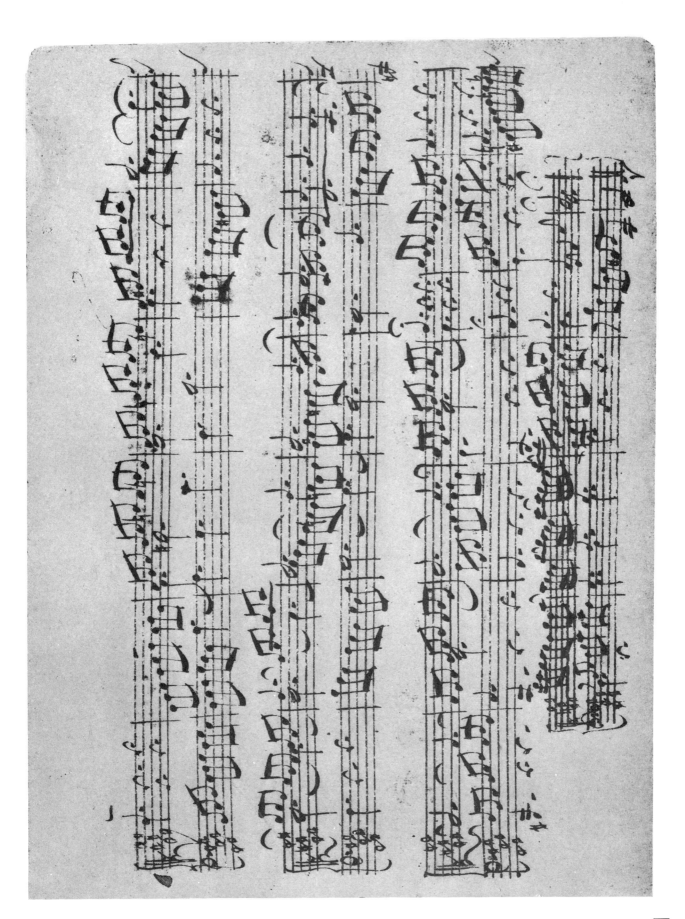

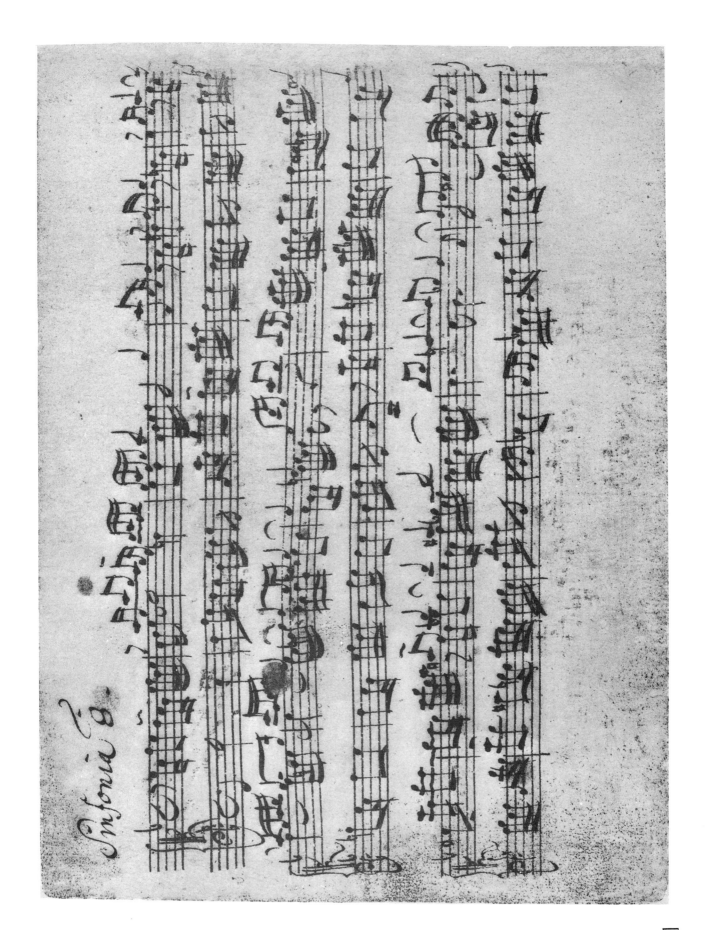

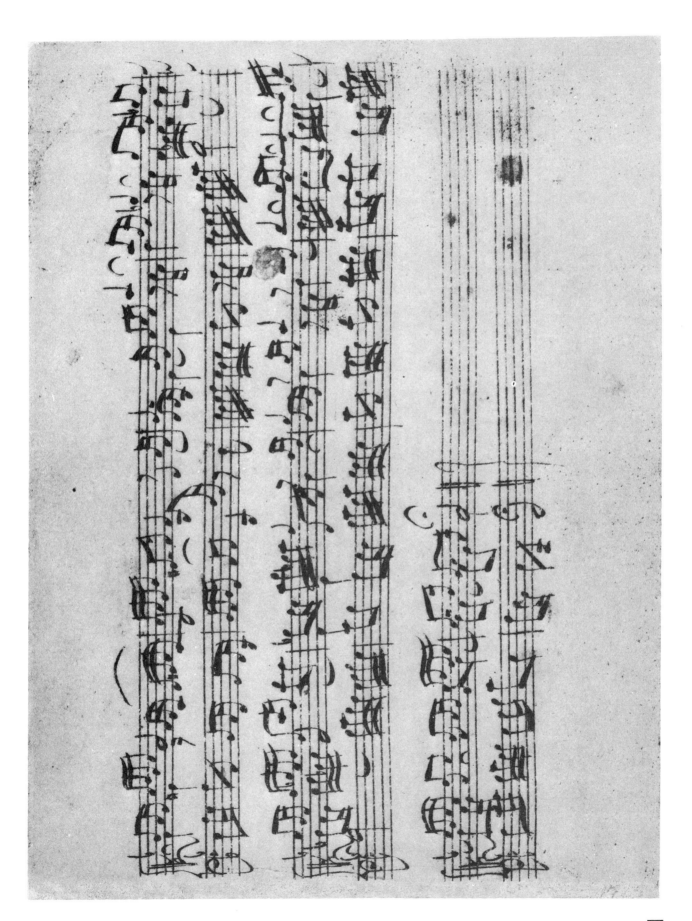

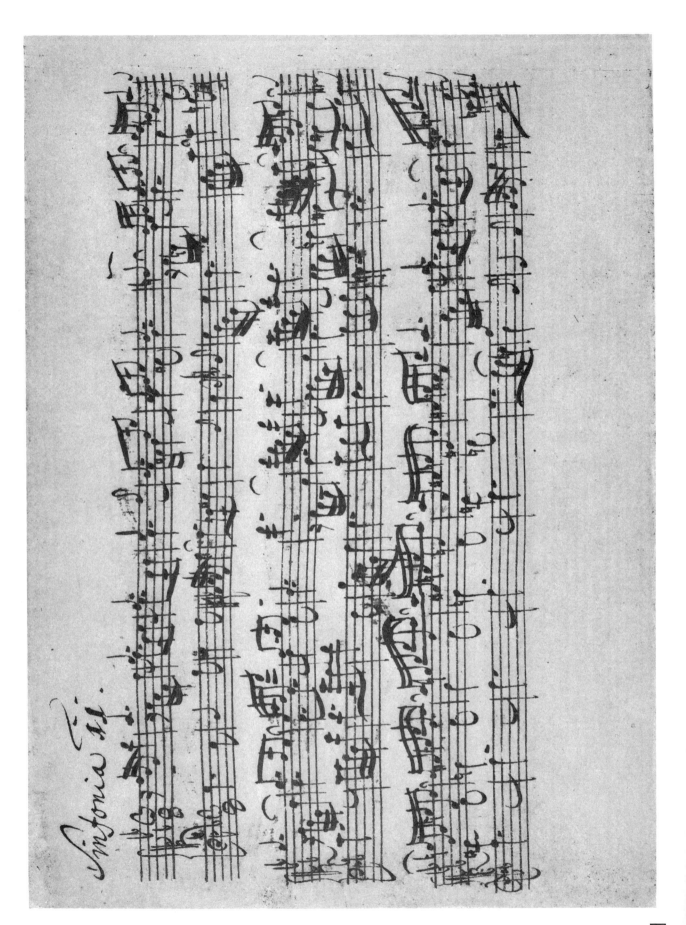

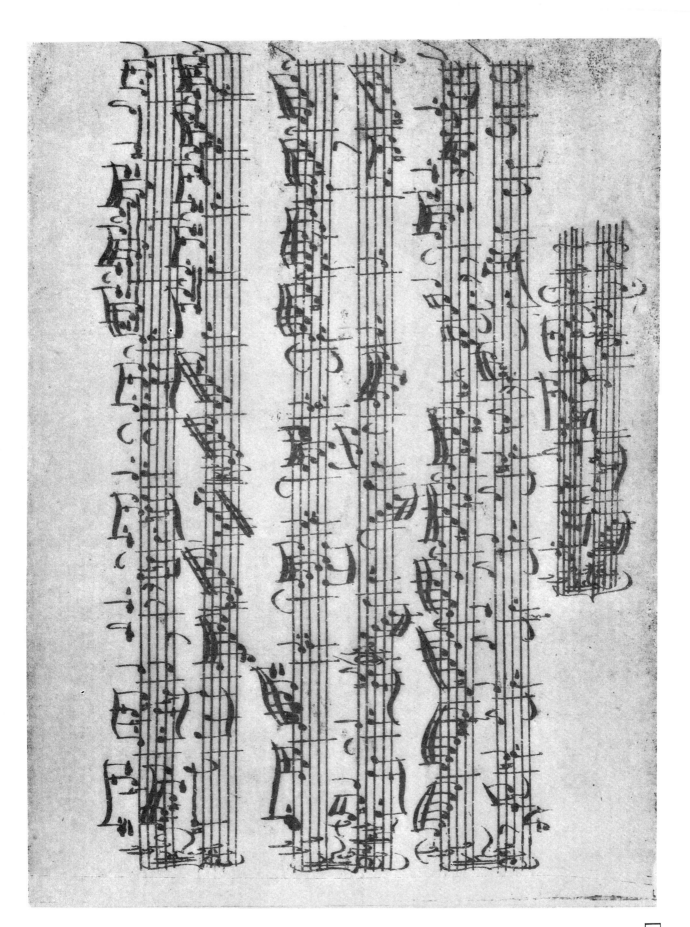

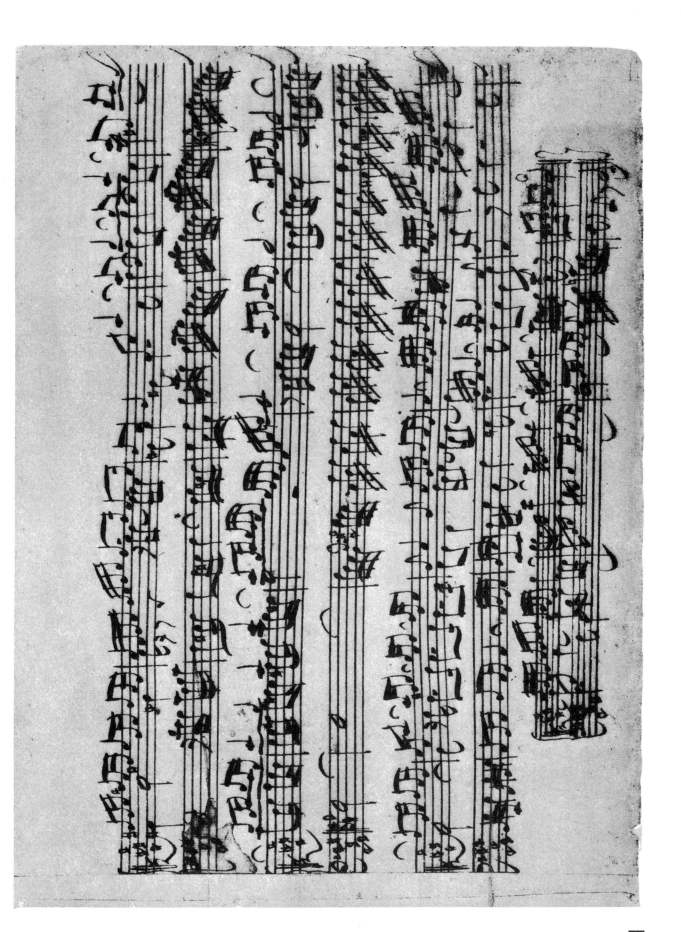

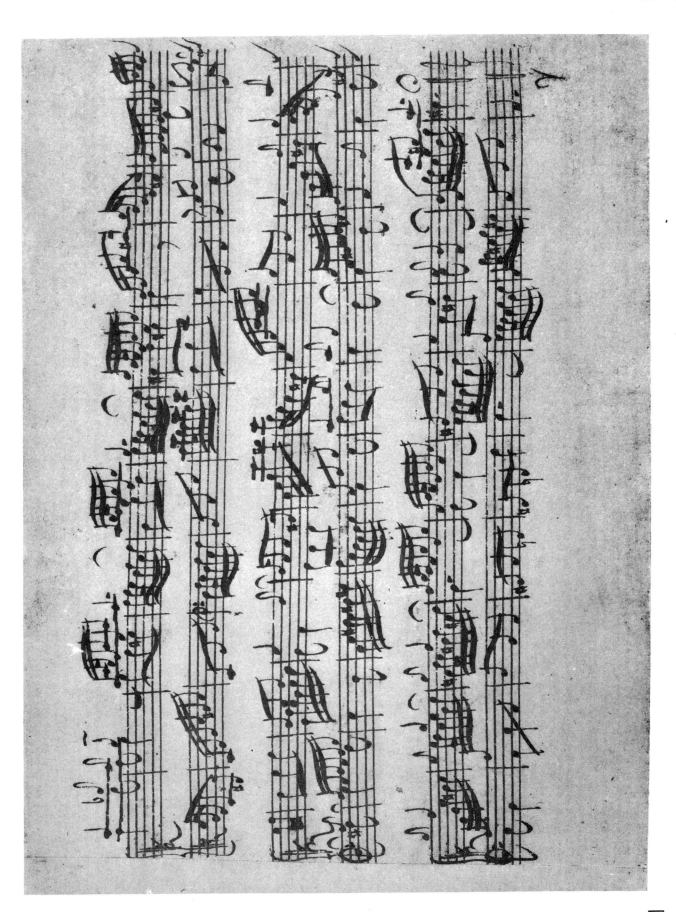

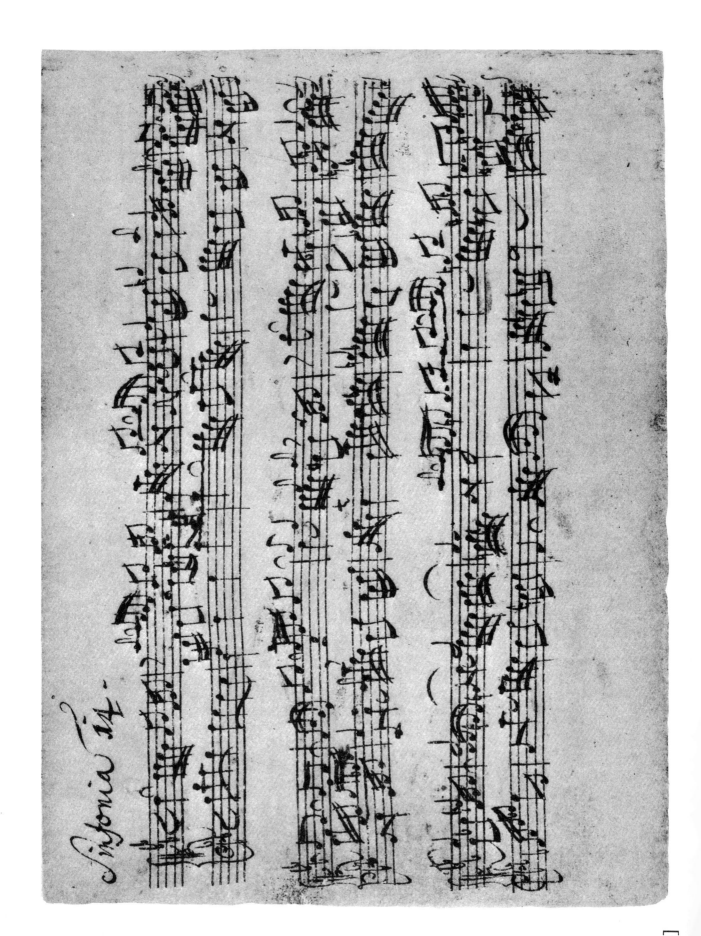

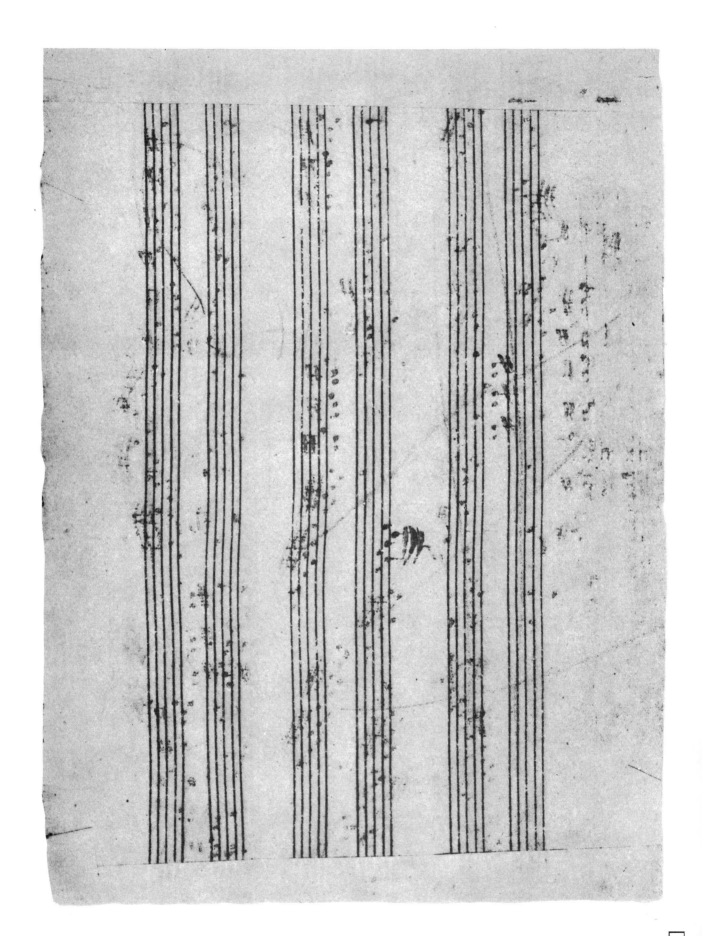